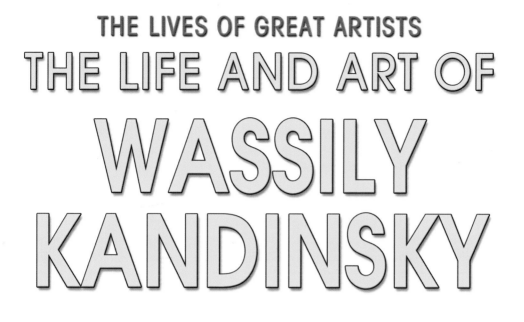

THE LIVES OF GREAT ARTISTS

THE LIFE AND ART OF

WASSILY KANDINSKY

THE LIVES OF GREAT ARTISTS

THE LIFE AND ART OF

WASSILY KANDINSKY

ANNABEL HOWARD

ROSEN
PUBLISHING®

New York

This edition published in 2017 by

The Rosen Publishing Group, Inc.
29 East 21st Street
New York, NY 10010

Library of Congress Cataloging-in-Publication Data

Names: Howard, Annabel, author. | Simpson, Adam, illustrator.

Title: The life and art of Wassily Kandinsky / Annabel Howard; illustrations by Adam Simpson.

Description: New York, NY : The Rosen Publishing Group, Inc., 2017. | Series:
 The lives of great artists | Includes bibliographical references and index.

Identifiers: LCCN 2016039105 | ISBN 9781499465822 (library bound)

Subjects: LCSH: Kandinsky, Wassily, 1866-1944—Juvenile literature. | Artists—Russia (Federation)—Biography—Juvenile literature.

Classification: LCC N6999.K33 H69 2019 | DDC 759.7 [B] —dc23

LC record available at https://lccn.loc.gov/2016039105

Manufactured in the United States of America

© Text 2015 Annabel Howard. Annabel Howard has asserted her right, under the Copyright, Designs, and Patent Act 1988, to be identified as the Author this Work.

© Illustrations 2015 Adam Simpson

Series editor: Catherine Ingram

This book was produced and published in 2015 by Laurence King Publishing Ltd., London.

Acknowledgments

I would like to thank Donald Dinwiddie for his creativity and his sharp eye, Adam Simpson for making the book what it is, and my husband D.W. for filling in the spaces I left vacant whilst writing this book.

About the Author

Annabel Howard has a degree in Art History from Christ Church, Oxford, and a Masters in Biographical Writing from the University of East Anglia. She h. taught and lectured in museums throughout the United Kingdom and Italy, and has contributed articles to magazines including Glass, World of Interiors, and The White Review.

About the Illustrator

Adam Simpson has contributed to major exhibitions in London, New York, Edinburgh, Bologna, and Japan. His work has been shortlisted for an Elle Decoration British Design Award and in 2009 he was included in the Art Directors Club Young Guns awards. Recent projects include artworks for BAFTA Conran, and a stamp commemorating the London Olympics.

Photo credits

All illustrations by Adam Simpson

6 © Heritage Image Partnership Ltd/Alamy; 11 © Artothek; 14 © Blauel/Gnamm/Artothek; 19 © Artothek; 20 Christie's Images, London/Scala, Florence; 29 © Christie's Images Ltd/Artothek; 31 akg-images/© DACS 2014; 37 © Artothek; 38 © Peter Willi/Artothek; 41 © Hans Hinz/Artothek; 42 & 45 © Artothek; 48 © Interfoto/Alamy; 49 © Artothek; 53 Photo © Centre Pompidou, MNAM-CCI, Dist. RMN-Grand Palais / Philippe Migeat; 56 The Solomon R. Guggenheim Foundation/Solomon R. Guggenheim Museum, New York/Art Resource, NY/ The Art Archive/© Hattula Moholy-Nagy/DACS 2014; 57 akg-images; 60 Maurice Babey/akg-images 64 The Solomon R. Guggenheim Foundation/Solomon R. Guggenheim Museum, New York/Art Resource, N'] The Art Archive; 65 © DACS 2014; 69 © Matteo Bazzi/epa european pressphoto agency b.v./Alamy; 70 Digital image, The Museum of Modern Art, New York/Scala, Florence/© DACS 2014; 73 The Solomon R. Guggenheim Foundation/Solomon R. Guggenheim Museum, New York/Art Resource, NY/The Ar Archive; 74-5 akg-images; 77 © Blauel/Gnamm/ Artothek; 81 Private Collection/Roger-Viollet, Paris/ Bridgeman Images.

Contents

Portait of Kandinsky in middle age
Photographer unknown

Kandinsky falls short of almost any image or stereotype of the artist. To look at he was tall and broad, stood very erect, and wore a pince-nez that gave him a mildly priggish air.

Born in Moscow, he grew up speaking three languages and became a man who existed more or less without national boundaries, travelling across the world and claiming citizenship in Russia, Germany, and France.

He was most comfortable wearing a suit, and it was often remarked in his later life that he looked rather bland, something like a businessman or an academic. He wouldn't have disagreed. He liked the image of himself as officiator – the sensitive but impartial judge – and believed himself to be something of a rational romantic. He also saw himself as the relic of an honourable past, a sensitive and honourable *belle époque* gentleman.

Underneath his calm façade was a deeply sensitive mind, prone to mysticism and poetry, that saw the "secret soul... not only in the stars, the moon, woods, and flowers... but even in a cigar butt lying in an ashtray, a patent white trouser-button... a submissive piece of bark... the page of a calendar."

Kandinsky's sensitivity combined with forceful yet contradictory elements of control and creativity to generate not only the man, but also some of the best painting of the modern era. It is why he has been described as one of the most important painters of the twentieth century.

The "Red Spot"

Russia was crucial to Kandinsky's identity and to his art. Despite an
almost life-long exile – initially self-imposed, then later enforced
by the authorities – Kandinsky clung to his Russian heritage.
He regarded Russia and particularly Moscow with a
mixture of nostalgia, longing, and fabulist romance.
He described the evening sun that dipped
over Moscow and dissolved the entire city
into a single red spot that, "like a wild
tuba, set all one's soul vibrating." He
also wrote that:

"To paint this hour,
I thought, must be for
an artist the most
impossible, the
greatest joy."

Siberia and Fairy Tales

Kandinsky's obsession with Moscow and his fantastical, dreamy vision of Russia had its roots in the romance of his family history. The Kandinskys had been exiled to Kyakhta, eastern Siberia (on the northern border with Mongolia) as punishment for agitation in the Decembrist Uprising of 1825. Wassily (or Basil) told stories about his ancestors, in particular one he described as a Mongolian princess. According to Kandinsky's fantastical tale, this ancestor rode to Russia on a miniature charger festooned with thousands of tiny bells, over enchanted Asian mountains which looked like porcelain.

Kandinsky's father was the first of the family to migrate back to Moscow, where he carved out a successful career as a tea merchant. In Moscow he met the renowned beauty and intellect Lidia Ivanovna Tikheyeva, whom he married. They settled in Moscow and, in 1866, Lidia gave birth to their only child, Wassily. The family was prosperous, cultured, and glamorous, and the little boy was adored: his parents took him to Venice, Florence, Rome, the Caucasus, and the Crimean Peninsula; they taught him the piano and the cello; they let him paint.

Kandinsky's maternal grandmother was Baltic German, and throughout his childhood she and his aunt read him traditional German fairy tales. The stories conjured fantastical images in the little boy's imagination. He stored them for over 20 years, and when he began painting, they were his primary source of inspiration. His most successful early works, like *Couple Riding,* depict romanticized images from German folklore. The presence of symbols – particularly the horse – as well as stories from folk and fairy tales are visible through his whole corpus.

Couple Riding
Wassily Kandinsky, 1906
Oil on canvas, 55 x 50 cm (21½ x 19½ in)
Städtische Galerie im Lenbachhaus und Kunstbau, Munich

The Seriousness of Youth

Kandinsky relied on his aunt and grandmother because, in 1871, his mother left. He was just five when his father moved the family to Odessa, on the Black Sea. Vassily's mother hated it and the move became the catalyst for the final breakdown of the marriage. Despite his mother's absence he idolized her, and her memory became intricately linked with his pulsing, wistful memories of Moscow.

Kandinsky became a sweet-natured, if whimsical boy, both observant and self-contained. He later wrote that as a child he suffered from anxiety, nightmares, and depression. He recalled how art offered some relief – as he described it: "[painting] lifted me out of time and space... so that I no longer felt myself."

Despite his obvious powers of imagination, Kandinsky did not pursue a creative path. He bowed to social and familial pressure, as well as the draw that his prodigious intellect offered his ambition, and chose to study law in Moscow. By the age of twenty-seven he was an associate professor with a promising future and a suitable young wife, his cousin Anya Tschimiakin. He was immaculately dressed in well-tailored suits, a neat moustache, and short, trimmed beard. Behind his wire-framed spectacles he was self-possessed to the point of rigidity.

Adventure

Kandinsky's choice of law set him up for a respectable and secure life. However, he continued to flirt with more creative and esoteric interests. Besides law and economics, Kandinsky also studied ethnography. In 1889, three years before he married Anya, he won a scholarship for a research trip to Vologda Oblast, a vast region over 373 miles (600 km) northeast of Moscow. Officially, he was to study the criminal jurisprudence and religion of the peoples who lived just below the Ural Mountains. Unofficially, he was chasing adventure and a romanticized vision of peasant life.

Anya accompanied him for the first leg of the journey. He left her at the town of Vologda and proceeded alone by train, steamer, and coach on a gruelling journey he recorded with some chagrin in his journal. Despite the physical discomfort, Kandinsky's observations are rich and poetic. He noted a sensation of adventuring through "another planet" – one of "unending forests and brightly coloured hills."

The mystical bent in his thinking can be partly ascribed to the *Kalevala* – an ancient Finnish epic containing semi-mystical tragedies and romances, tales of witchcraft, heroism, and betrayal. He read it as he travelled and the poems opened his eyes to layers of possibility in the landscape. Like the fairy tales of his childhood, the images that his imagination created imprinted themselves deeply in his mind and they reappeared years later in early paintings like *Golden Sail* (see p.12).

During the trip Kandinsky matured. The endearing enthusiasm and excitement exhibited at the beginning of his journal is gradually replaced by a real awareness of the punishing reality of life outside his privileged upbringing. For the first time Kandinsky learnt the value of a hot meal, and the discomfort of hunger. He noted with some regret that there was no local word for wife, only "woman," and he was deeply shocked by the poverty he saw. "Everything is quiet," he wrote, "and infinitely poor. Everywhere poverty, poverty."

Golden Sail

Wassily Kandinsky, 1903

Woodcut, 12.7 x 29.7 cm (5 x 11½ in)

Städtische Galerie im Lenbachhaus und Kunstbau, Munich

Perception

In Vologda, Kandinsky spent most of his time with the impoverished and reviled Zyrian people. When he returned to Moscow he bravely declared that he had "fallen in love with them… despite the fact that everyone slanders them." Around this time, Kandinsky began profoundly to question accepted social norms.

The trip also proved a turning point. He wasn't painting but the aesthetic orientation of his responses is recorded in his diary. The local colours astonished him; the people appeared to him as "brightly coloured living pictures on two legs." His impression of the local houses stayed with him for the rest of his life; he saw them as "wonderhouses," like "painted folksongs… a miracle." Inside these houses he said he truly learnt how to enter a picture. He spent his artistic life trying to recreate this feeling of absorption, to create work that was powerful enough to force the spectator to abandon themselves, to walk out of their terrestrial reality into a spiritual realm conjured with paint.

Confusion and Change

After the trip to Vologda, Kandinsky settled down to his life and career. His success as a professor of law continued and, in 1896, at the age of twenty-nine, he was offered a tenure position at the famous department in the University of Dorpat (now Tartu) in Estonia. He turned it down. Instead he quit and, as a means of escape, took a job running the N. Kusverev print factory in Moscow.

Over the next year two events propelled Kandinsky away from the rational certainties of his young life. The faith he'd placed in jurisprudence and logic had already begun to seem misguided when radioactivity was discovered. Kandinsky, who was extremely well informed about and interested in science wrote:

> The disintegration of the atom was equal in my soul to the disintegration of the whole world. Suddenly the thickest walls fell. Everything became uncertain, wobbly and soft… science seemed to me destroyed, its most important basis was only a madness.

Kandinsky started to search for different answers. They coalesced at an art exhibition in 1896. Here he encountered a painting that confused and intrigued him: it appeared to have no subject matter so he turned to the catalogue, but after reading its description he still could not discern an object on the canvas. He was surprised to discover that his pleasure in the painting was undiminished. Here he found a different kind of answer than that he'd searched for, and not found, in science and law. He later wrote that in those moments:

> Painting acquired a new fairy-tale power and splendour…

> I had the impression that a small part of my fairy-tale Moscow already existed on the canvas.

The painting that impressed Kandinsky was Monet's *Haystacks*. Months after he saw it he left the print factory and his treasured Moscow and started his life afresh in Germany.

Kandinsky Reborn

Kandinsky chose Munich – a city that, in the words of novelist Thomas Mann, was at that time "radiant" with art. It was a creative centre where, Kandinsky recalled, "everyone painted – or wrote poems, or made music, or took up dancing." It was the perfect location to begin his life afresh. Munich was buzzing, and so was Kandinsky, who described himself as "reborn." With the aid of financial support from his generous and supportive father, he enrolled in a private art school, and embraced a completely new life.

Kandinsky was an inherently diligent person, but during the first two years in Munich he found himself attending art school less and less often. In the eyes of his teachers he was a proficient but unexceptional student. In general they considered his palette too bright, and his drawing skills weak. Their criteria for judgement were dictated by a formal academic system and a staid public. Munich's deeply conservative art world was ripe for change, and Kandinsky was primed to lead the revolution.

Although he was frustrated as a student, Kandinsky did not rant or rail. In a typically restrained act of rebellion, he simply left the conservative confines of the school, and went off to paint subjects of his own choice, in his own style, and on his own terms. He wasn't a natural rebel, and found it hard to abandon the idea of the institution. He doggedly applied himself to academic painting and drawing, weathering rejections, and persisting in an attempt to win respect from the Munich Academy, where he was accepted as a student in 1900, after an earlier failed entrance exam.

One year later, Kandinsky felt qualified to strike out on his own. Using his prodigious organizational skills and energy he founded Phalanx, a movement which aimed to overthrow the academic style and the staid theories of official art. Kandinsky envisaged himself and his like-minded artists as an army crusading into the intellectual unknown, against the forces of academic conservatism (see image p. 17).

Munich

The fact that in a little less than four years Kandinsky morphed from a student into the founder of an art movement is a testament to his energy, as well as to his marked confidence and natural authority. Phalanx was primarily an exhibiting society. It aimed to combat the traditional and restrictive system of art submissions, breaking free of stylistic restriction and – refreshingly – sexual inequality. Between 1901 and 1904 Phalanx (and therefore Kandinsky) organized 12 exhibitions. The poster for the first exhibition, which opened on August 17, 1901, shows a phalanx – a formation of Greek soldiers, a symbol chosen by Kandinsky for its typically romantic and mythical associations – represented by two figures, one male one female, charging through the Bavarian landscape.

In late 1901 Kandinksy, not content with the mammoth task of organizing the exhibition, decided also to open a Phalanx school. "With characteristic daring and little forethought" he found a large studio building at Hohenzollernstrasse in Schwabing, the Bohemian quarter of Munich. Kandinsky had a natural aptitude for teaching and, throughout his artistic career, both theory and the communication of aesthetic ideas formed an important part of his artistic life and development. From the very beginning his students noted his generosity and power to inspire. He quickly attracted a greater following than his more experienced and well-known colleagues. One of his acolytes was a determined and talented young lady named Gabriele Münter who described his pedagogy as "encouraging and individual."

Poster for the Phalanx Exhibition

Wassily Kandinsky, 1901

Lithograph, 45.5 x 58.9 cm (18 x 23 in)

Städtische Galerie im Lenbachhaus und Kunstbau, Munich

The Singer
Wassily Kandinsky, 1903

Woodcut, 20 x 14.8 cm (8 x 6 in)
Private collection

Music and Inspiration

A proficient cellist and pianist, Kandinsky became a close follower of musical developments in Munich. He found that music elicited very intense responses from him and provided both sublime escape and visual stimulus. He described music as "the ultimate teacher," and one of his most famous quotes reads:

> Colour is the keyboard, the eyes are the hammers, the soul is the piano with many strings. The artist is the hand which plays, touching one key or another, to cause vibrations in the soul.

Even so, nothing prepared him for what he heard in 1897 when he went to the production of a relatively modern piece: Wagner's *Lohengrin*.

> I saw all the colours in my mind; they stood before my eyes. Wild, almost crazy lines were sketched in front of me... Wagner had painted "my hour" musically.

The piece was, for him, the musical evocation of the Moscow dusk that was his greatest inspiration, and he saw it as clearly as if it had already been painted.

Kandinsky's response to Wagner revealed to him an aesthetic path. What enabled him to start on this path was experimentation with a new technique: woodcutting. The technique, which required a simplicity of form and line, constituted a shrinkage of form down to what he began to call "inner necessity." More than that though, carving the wood created in him a visceral reaction that resulted in a feeling akin to ecstasy. When he cut into the grain he felt as though "music rang in my whole body and God was in my heart." It is perhaps not a coincidence that a number of his woodcuts, like *The Singer,* take up musical themes.

Synaesthesia

Kandinsky's responses to both *Lohengrin* and to Monet's *Haystacks* were unusually powerful, even for an artist. Years later, he wrote of the *Haystacks*: "[it] impressed itself indelibly on my memory and constantly floated before my eyes, quite unexpectedly, complete in every detail."

One explanation for these reactions is neurological. Kandinsky experienced a condition known as synaesthesia. This phenomenon manifests itself in many different forms and is still little understood. One of its principal manifestations is that stimulus of one sense receptor produces more than one simultaneous sensory reaction. For example, a synaesthete would, like everyone else, perceive the number seven as black lines that convey a meaning. They would also, however, experience the letter as a colour, a texture, or even a sound. This is not something that the synaesthete can control, it is inherent to their experience of the world. In Kandinsky's case, music resonated most strongly, and throughout his life he describes the vivid colours and images drawn on his mind's eye by sound.

The way that Kandinksy's brain recoursed to colour was integral to his way of thinking about, remembering, and perceiving the world. His memory was extraordinarily vivid and enduring, and he could often recall incidents from his distant past because they focused around a colour that particularly attracted or repelled him. For example, he told the story of the family coachman who, when Kandinsky was three or four, stripped tree branches to make "horses" for him to play with. The branches were thin and black and when cut they revealed a brownish yellow that Kandinsky disliked intensely. The inner layer of the stem, however, he loved, because it was a juicy green, and he recalled how the deepest layer brought the branch to life with an ivory colour that conjured up a "happy smell, that made me want to lick it." From the very beginning, in Kandinsky's world, each colour "live[d] by its own mysterious inner life."

The Path Diverges

In the summer of 1902 Kandinsky organized a painting trip with some of his students from Phalanx. They journeyed south to the lower reaches of the Bavarian Alps and spent a few weeks painting in the countryside around Kochel. It was a blissful time. Kandinsky painted, wrote, walked, joked with, and entertained, his students. There was one student in particular who inspired his lightness of mood: Gabriele Münter.

Initially, Münter seems to have been unaware of Kandinsky's growing affection; she wrote in her reminiscences that she was "naïve" and a "goose" for not realizing where their relationship was headed. Their increasing intimacy was, however, becoming obvious to everyone else. The only two who owned bicycles, they would go for long rides into the mountains together, and Münter later recalled how they would grab one another's handle bars until they toppled over, and how every so often she would joyfully and indecorously break into song and dance when they were walking.

There was no physical intimacy, but the bond was obvious enough that when Anya came to join her husband, Kandinsky introduced the two women and then suddenly, the next day, asked Münter to leave. Despite the fact that her painting was just beginning to take off, Münter packed her things and disappeared without a protest.

A Battle for Honour

The story, however, was only just beginning. Kandinsky and Münter continued to write to one another, and in Munich that autumn they shared their first kiss. Münter was confused and full of conflict. She was elated, but also alarmed – and fully aware of the danger in this liaison. In a particularly revealing letter (which she never sent, but which became a diary entry), she laments how she'd always dreamt of a "cosy and harmonious" happiness, of loving someone who "wholly & always belongs to me." She wrote of how she despised secrecy, and could not endure the idea of a hidden tryst. She also, however, admitted to herself that she'd be prepared to sacrifice her every expectation to be a part of a life with Kandinsky. In a prescient paragraph near the end of the note she concluded: "Kandinsky, let me have my peace of mind again!"

Kandinsky was equally disturbed, although less by fears of the future, than by Münter's apparent lack of interest. He showered her with letters throughout October and November and, unlike her, constantly declared his affection, writing that he had lost his equanimity and that he thought only of her.

A second preoccupation also emerges through their letters. Kandinsky was concerned for his self-image. He regarded himself as upright and honourable, and at one point called for a "tiny bit of character!... Even though it hurts." He wanted to do the right thing by Anya, even though he could not disguise his infatuation with Münter from her or anybody else. It left him with a conundrum that he took out in self-recrimination.

Ever the fair and dispassionate judge in other people's affairs, when it came to his own life, he failed to see how deeply his actions affected other people (and not just Anya). This blindness was something that Münter only became aware of years later, at an enormous cost to her happiness, even her sanity.

Turmoil

In 1903 Kandinsky and Anya quietly agreed to give up any marital or emotional claims on one other and Kandinsky and Münter – discreetly but finally – became lovers. During that summer's painting expedition, this time to the medieval city of Kallmünz, they famously celebrated their "engagement." Although Kandinsky declared himself dizzyingly happy, his sense of propriety had left him with a heavy burden of guilt. He was restless and despondent, lacking confidence in his work as well as in himself. His core belief in his artistic future never faltered (in 1904 he wrote: "If destiny will grant me enough time, I shall discover a new international language that will endure forever"). The problem was that he could no longer see his path.

In later years Anya, Wassily, and even Münter remained close friends – no mean feat. In some way Kandinsky had remained the gentleman of honour. Even so, there is an inescapable sense that despite his good intentions, he was blind and single-minded in his pursuit of Münter, and thought more of himself than of the women whose lives he was irreparably transforming.

Escape

Hard as he tried, through the remaining months of 1903 and through most of 1904, Kandinsky could not find the "international language" he was seeking. His answer to the emotional, artistic, and social pressure was to escape. Towards the end of 1904 – aged 38 – he finally abandoned Anya, his house, and many of his possessions and set off, with his "fiancée" Münter, directionless. They went to Tunisia where they stayed for a few months. Then they travelled to Carthage, and via Italy back to Munich and, shortly after, to Dresden and Milan. They ranged over Europe, stopping off for a few months at a time. They went to Rapallo and to Paris, moving just outside the city to Sèvres where they stayed for a year.

During this time, Kandinsky saw the work of, among others, Henri Matisse, Pablo Picasso, Raoul Dufy, and "le Douanier" Rousseau. He was both inspired and overwhelmed by the sheer strength and breadth of their vision. In February 1907, he asked Münter to leave him – claiming that he needed time alone. As soon as she left, however, he wrote to tell her that he was lonely, self-doubting, and miserable. He confessed that when he got home from putting her on the train he broke down in tears of anguish and "tore my hair and wept so wildly I was afraid the landlord would come."

From a man with such enduring self-control this period was obviously one of deep distress. Münter later recalled how he would sometimes cry out from sheer nervous energy, and how he suffered from headaches, dizziness, and despair. By the time the pair reunited for the last leg of their journey – to Switzerland – they were mentally and physically overwrought. Kandinsky checked himself into a spa, where he spent five weeks recuperating. The "trial period" of their relationship had been an exhausting four years on the road, and both were ready to settle down. From Switzerland they journeyed to Berlin and then, finally, home to Munich.

Theosophy and Metaphysics

A black, E white, I red, U green, O blue: vowels. . .
(Rimbaud)

As he travelled, Kandinsky broke through more and more of his bourgeois and self-imposed mental parameters. His brain was a receiving ground not only for art but also for ideas, and Paris, where the couple spent a year, was full of them. In particular he was drawn to the literary and artistic work of the French Symbolists: a group of poets and artists who reacted against the rationalism and materialism of the nineteenth century and instead escaped to a world of subjectivity and suggestion. The Symbolists prioritized experience over representation, and veiled objects with ambiguity and displacement. Their ideas encouraged Kandinsky to start making pithy yet elusive statements such as: "Speaking of the hidden by means of the hidden. Is this not content?" The Symbolists' talk of art as a form of redemption – a moral vehicle – was also important. It appealed strongly to Kandinsky, a man who shied away from art for the first half of his adult life because he felt an obligation to society and to Russia.

His exploration of ideas stretched far beyond a dalliance with avant-garde art and a belief in moral purpose, though. At this time he became interested in a strand of mysticism that was emerging, not only in Paris, but across the industrialized world. He became especially interested in theosophy – a nineteenth-century attempt to channel all known religion into a common system. His notebooks include passages copied from articles by the leading theosophist Rudolf Steiner, most of which concern "Man's Aura."

Although there is no evidence that Kandinsky ever subscribed to theosophical beliefs, there is no doubt that a great deal of his time and attention was devoted to mysticism. Later in his life he was often referred to as "spiritual," and Münter called him "a holy man." He believed in faith healing, and his occult library was substantial, including books on esoteric philosophy, meditation, and the paranormal. He was particularly interested in "thought photography," or the idea that thoughts could be captured in the form of images. One of these books was *Thought Forms* by prominent theosophists Annie Besant and Charles Leadbeater. In it the authors outlined the forms and colours of various "thoughts" created by emotions or stimuli such as music. The visual link between images like *Music of Gounod* and Kandinsky's early abstract work is evident.

ate G, Music of Gounod

m Thought Forms by Annie Besant
d C. W. Leadbeater, 1901.

The Great Leap Forward

In the spring of 1908 Kandinsky and Münter were in Munich, but living apart and not entirely settled. They went on regular hiking expeditions through the foothills of the Bavarian Alps, and on one of these they discovered the old market town of Murnau. They raved about it with such enthusiasm to their friends – fellow expatriate Russians Alexj von Jawlensky and Marianne von Werefkin – that the couple rented a house there for a couple of months. In August, Kandinsky and Münter joined them, and under the late summer sun the two couples painted together for three weeks. All four painted with inspired fury. Kandinsky, who described himself in his life before art as "like a monkey caught in a net," was finally, gloriously, free. What he had found was colour. Having finally managed to process the Fauve work that he'd seen in Paris, he combined its influence with his interest in theosophy to produce intuitive, riotous, and expressive landscapes, like *Autumn Landscape with Boats* (1908). This was the first step that Kandinsky took towards finding what he described as his spiritual language.

Even when Kandinsky and Münter weren't painting, Murnau provided inspiration, and not only in its natural beauty. Local art – and particularly the unusual *Hinterglasmalerei* (reverse glass painting) – proved to be a strong influence. Münter described that summer: "After a period of agony, I took a great leap forward – from copying nature – to feeling the content of things – abstracting – conveying the abstract." She may as well have been speaking for Kandinsky.

Glass Painting with the Sun
Wassily Kandinsky, 1910

Glass painting, 30.6 x 40.3 cm (12 x 16 in)
Städtische Galerie im Lenbachhaus und Kunstbau, Munich

Breakthrough

Through the last months of 1908 and into 1909, the four friends built on the successful summer of painting. In January they formed the New Artists' Association Munich (NKVM), and began preparing for exhibitions. The group attracted a great deal of young talent, and Jawlensky's studio in Munich's bohemian Schwabing quarter became a renowned seat for discussions about new directions for art.

During this period Kandinsky was alive to stimulus. Still embroiled in the battle to produce "true" art, he was nevertheless ecstatic and had found his language and his path. In the spring he and Münter returned to Murnau, and Kandinsky persuaded her to buy a house there. Although they filled it with local art and traditional furniture, it was from the very beginning referred to as "the Russian house." This wasn't far from the truth: they painted the window frames, stairs, and tables so that Kandinsky was finally able to recreate his own version of the "living canvas" that so inspired him in Vologda.

Both painters also worked hard on their own development. They started to produce their own *Hinterglasmalerei* – for example *Glass Painting with the Sun*. Experimentation with a different technique once again unleashed a fresh spontaneity of form, a new purity of colour, and an economy of line that helped Kandinsky to reduce the dominance of the object and let his palette sing.

Gabriele Münter
*Kandinsky and Erma Bossi
at the Table in the Murnau
House,* 1912
Oil on canvas, 95.5 x 125.5 cm
(37½ x 49½ in)
Städtische Galerie im Lenbachhaus
und Kunstbau, Munich

The Nut and Its Shell

Part of Kandinsky's way out of the monkey's net had been writing, and throughout this period his aesthetic creativity was matched only by his intellectual outpourings. He may have abandoned academia and renounced science, but he was a thinker and a writer, and never lost the urge to reason through words, so he began to write.

His overriding and principal theme was truth. He saw art as accessing truth through a series of "sudden illuminations, like lightning, or explosions, which burst like fireworks in the heavens." This truth relates to *inner experience* – something which, for a logical man, initially seems a deeply irrational and subjective standpoint.

It was. Kandinsky had abandoned the hard lines of science and logic. "Nothing is absolute," he wrote in 1912. Kandinsky felt he had broken through the "nightmare of materialism, which has turned the life of the universe into an evil, useless game." Art became his moral conviction.

"This motion in truth is very complicated: the untrue becomes true, the true becomes untrue, some parts fall off like the shell from a nut, time smoothes this shell; for this reason some mistake the shell for the nut, and bestow on this shell the life of the nut; many fight over the shell and the nut rolls on."

– from Kandinsky's *Concerning the Spiritual in Art.*

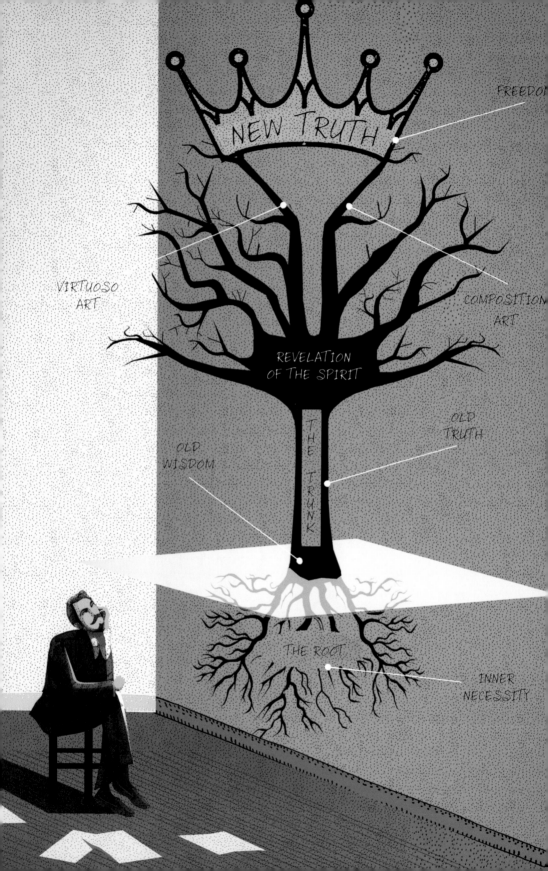

Concerning the Spiritual in Art

As his writing evolved, Kandinsky began to depict the artist as a prophet, poised to pull humanity up through the murk of ignorance to the higher plain of truth. He used many metaphors to explain his ideas, but one of his most emblematic is that of the tree. He visualized the tree as a bridge between the unenlightened, profane mass of humanity, still fixed on an outdated "old truth," and the freedom that can be accessed through true enlightenment. Kandinsky was convinced that it was the artist's role to bring the greater mass of human consciousness towards this freedom, which would otherwise remain out of reach.

Kandinsky famously expressed his thoughts in what is publishing's least likely best seller, and one of the most influential books of art theory ever written. *Concerning the Spiritual in Art,* written at the end of 1911, was based on ideas that Kandinsky began to formulate in the summer of 1910, in Murnau. The book is a coherent and profound exploration of abstraction. Although other artists were exploring similar ideas in their art, Kandinksy was the one who realized their full implications and communicated them to thousands of people through his writing. His book argues for an art that moves beyond articulate ideas and does not rely on references to nature for its content. It urged artists to create work based solely on the sensation and perception of colour and form. It also stipulated, however, that the artist's vision must be based on an "inner necessity" (a term that Kandinsky uses more or less interchangeably with "inner truth").

This "inner necessity" is what Kandinsky felt had been lost to the rapaciousness and speed of nineteenth-century materialism. Without it, no artist's work could be great. He felt that, "the artist must train not only his eye but also his soul," and that without an understanding of "inner necessity" the work produced would be "mere decoration… suited to neckties or carpets."

It never occurred to Kandinsky, either in the early 1900s, or much later, through both World Wars and all their concomitant trauma, that "spiritual" progress might not, over time, lead humanity from a limited and inflexible state towards one of truth. It was the intensity of his belief that allowed him to make the first great leaps towards a new way of thinking.

New Friends, New Ideas

At the end of 1910 Kandinsky was still alive to new stimuli. In October he went on an overdue trip home to Russia. From Moscow he wrote to Münter: "Why is life here… more intense, more gripping?… Moscow is – whiplash, Moscow is – balm."

By the end of the year he was back, and he met the young Franz Marc at Jawlensky's New Year's Eve party. Amid a chorus of howling abuse, Marc had written the only supportive review of that autumn's NKVM exhibition. Their rapport was immediate and their respect mutual. Marc wrote to his lover Maria Frank the next day that: "When it comes to personal charm, Kandinsky outshines them all… I was totally captivated by the man." Kandinsky for his part immediately invited Marc to a concert that was taking place the next day.

The concert featured the Munich premiere of Arnold Schoenberg's second string quartet. The music shocked the Munich audience with its atonality and its whimsical lyrics, such as, "I feel the air of another planet." A large part of the audience hissed and laughed but, for Marc and Kandinsky, the music was a revelation. Here was a musician who, like them, challenged traditional models of harmony and coherence. Kandinsky rushed home, not to his books this time, but to his paints, and created *Impression III (Concert)*, in which a large black piano dominates the composition. The audience members lean towards it, and streaks and patches and blobs of colour emanate like some sort of meteor shower. The room has come alive.

What Kandinsky took from the evening was a confirmation of what he already knew: that it was possible to create a response in the viewer without an object or a story, and that you could do this while challenging the traditional form of your discipline.

He wrote to Schoenberg in a buzz of childish and breathless excitement. They weren't to meet for another eight months, but in the written friendship that developed, Kandinsky relaxed his usual reserve and peppered his writing with enthusiastic exclamation marks as well as constant and profoundly generous encouragement.

Composition IV

Wassily Kandinksy, 1911

Oil on canvas, 159.5 x 250.5 cm (63 x 98 in)
Kunstsammlung Nordrhein-Westfalen, Dusseldorf

Reaching for Abstraction

Despite the huge leaps that Kandinsky had taken – both intellectually and aesthetically – during the years leading up to 1910, his campaign was far from over. It never was. The battle was for truth, but the war was fought against himself, and so there could be no final resolution. Every time he crested a ridge or rounded a corner, he stretched himself a little further, set his goal slightly farther away. And so, in his own words, he felt at this time:

> Unable to separate the nucleus from the skin. I thought of a snake which did not quite succeed in crawling out of its old skin. The skin already looked so terribly dead – but it still clung…

Around 1910 there was, however a significant change: the first abstract painting. Kandinksy wrote that in 1910 he walked into his studio and, in the half-light of dusk, he saw a painting there so beautiful that it moved him to tears. The moment was fleeting – he soon realized that it was one of his own canvases, a sketch for *Composition IV* that Münter had turned on its side while tidying up the studio. It reminded him of his encounter with Monet; it finally liberated him from the object.

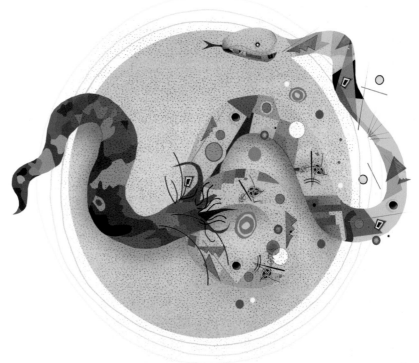

Abstraction

Exactly when Kandinsky painted his first abstract work, and whether or not he was the first abstract painter of the twentieth century, has been the subject of fierce debate. He was himself a vehement defender of his role in the development of Western painting, making nine written references to the fact that in 1910 he painted the first abstract painting – Kandinsky was an ambitious man.

Around this time the frenetic pace of Kandinsky's life started to take its toll on his relationship. He spent less time with Münter, who increasingly travelled, spending the entire summer of 1911 on an extended visit to her family. Their correspondence from this time begins to show signs of strain, with gripes from Münter mostly fended off with phlegmatic and evasive responses from Kandinsky. At one point, however, he apologized for making Münter's life "so unpleasant." In a melodramatic addendum, he wrote: "Years ago I seriously thought of going to Siberia and freeing the people I love from me. It would be better if these people were to abandon me and I were alone and could do no damage…"

An increasing self-sufficiency and independence begins to appear in his work from 1910. He almost exclusively made canvases titled *Impression*, *Improvisation,* and *Composition. Impressions* related to nature, and were the most spontaneous form. *Improvisations* captured experiences and emotions from Kandinsky's inner world, and *Compositions* were his symphonies: the culmination of his work and thought. He knew they were important; he said that the word "composition" alone filled him with reverence. He made his first in January 1910, but *Composition V*, finished in the same month that he published *Concerning the Spiritual in Art* (November 1911), was the first major canvas that was entirely abstract. And this was perhaps the reason why his friends at the NKVM rejected it from inclusion in their show that December.

Cover of catalogue for *The Blue Rider*

Wassily Kandinsky, 1911

27.9 x 21.9 cm (11 x 8½ in)

Städtische Galerie im Lenbachhaus und Kunstbau, Munich

The Blue Rider

Fissures had been emerging within the NKVM for some time, and the rejection of *Composition V* was the nail in the coffin of the group. Marc and Kandinsky were prepared: for about six months they'd been planning their next project – Der Blaue Reiter (The Blue Rider), a group of about a dozen artists who exhibited together. That was all. Kandinsky disingenuously claimed that he and Marc came up with the name spontaneously, over coffee, because he liked riders, Marc liked horses, and blue was the favourite colour of both of them.

The first exhibition was met with mute confusion, even by well-meaning critics. Viewers failed to see what connected the images on the walls, despite Kandinsky's unapologetic disclaimer which stated: "Our purpose is to show how the inner wish of the artist takes shape in manifold forms."

Important as the Blue Rider exhibitions were, it was Kandinsky and Marc's almanac – a compendium of essays, poems, songs, and an astoundingly broad range of images – that left a lasting mark on twentieth-century art. The almanac loosely presents a quest for spiritual truth, a battle against the crippling materialism of the Modern era. Some of the exhibiting artists helped to edit the almanac. The young August Macke was one. So was his close friend Paul Klee who, although not a man easily moved to praise, recorded his impression of Kandinsky as a man with: "an exceptionally beautiful and lucid mind."

Despite the enlightened support and encouragement of publicist Reinhard Piper, producing the almanac was no easy task. As Kandinsky himself wrote to Marc:

> I feel a little funny. Just like… well, like before an attractive, tremendously interesting mountain climb, but one where you have to crawl through crevasses and ride on ridges.

43

Apocalypse

The summer of 1911 was the fourth at Murnau. This time, however, Kandinsky spent much of it alone. It was a strange season. The weather was uncharacteristically warm. The sun shone every day, and Kandinsky spent a lot of time gardening and taking care of the orchard. Schoenberg's letters locate their common ground, "in what you call the 'unlogical' and I call the 'elimination of the conscious will in art.'" Kandinsky put this illogicality into a set of poems and woodcuts he was preparing for a book called *Klange* (*Sounds*, published in 1913). Thematically, the book revolves around perception, and, in particular, ideas of appearance and dissolution. He joked about the artist's relationship to the pen, saying that in the past artists' writings were admired and that painters were not "practically expected to eat with a brush rather than a fork." The book was hugely influential. The Dadaist and later Surrealist Hans (Jean) Arp, said of *Klange* when it was first published:

> These works breathe the secrets of eternal and unexplored depths. Forms arise, as powerful as talking mountains. Sulphur and poppy stars blossom on the lips of the sky.

In 1909 Kandinsky had attended a lecture by Rudolph Steiner, who talked of apocalypse, as had the Symbolists. Whether this was the seed of his growing unease, or whether it related to Münter or even a sense of the gathering storm over Europe, is unclear. Wherever it came from, it emerged strongly in his painting from 1911 to 1914. Both *Four Horsemen of the Apocalypse* and *Composition V* relate directly to apocalyptic themes.

Four Horsemen of the Apocalypse

Wassily Kandinsky, 1911

Tempera on glass, 29.5 x 20cm (11½ x 8 in)
Städtische Galerie im Lenbachhaus und Kunstbau, Munich

Crossing Borders

On August 1, 1914, the Germans declared war on Russia.
Kandinsky was thrown into a race against time to escape from
Germany, and he and Münter fled to neutral Switzerland. There
they rented a small cottage by Lake Contstance. They saw no one
– they appear to have been thrown into a form of shock. In early
November Kandinsky decided that it was time to return to Russia.

A World Turned Upside Down

The War altered everything for Kandinsky. It was not just the wider world that had changed: the physical and emotional landscape of his life was damaged beyond repair. In Murnau, he left behind his home, his friends, most of his possessions, his extensive art collection, and almost all of his own work. On August 2 he wrote to his gallerist and great supporter, Herwarth Walden:

> It is as though I'm thrown out of a dream… I've been torn out of this illusion. Mountains of corpses, frightful agonies of the most varied kind, inner culture set back for an indefinite time…

In Moscow the situation did not brighten. His father was living on reduced means in Odessa and, isolated in Russia, he lived a meagre existence. In 1913 he had sold his family home and commenced building a block of apartments on Dolgy Street. He moved into one of the apartments, but there was little reprieve and pervasive financial worry. News from the West was uniformly grim. Macke and Marc – two of Kandinsky's closest friends and artistic allies – were killed in the fighting.

In 1915 Kandinsky did not paint a single work in oil, his preferred medium for major works since the beginning of his career. He worked exclusively on paper until 1916, and the few paintings he did produce during that year and those that followed (up to 1919) retreat from the dangerous edge of abstraction. *Moscow: Red Square,* for example, takes the motifs from the seminal *Small Pleasures* (painted two years earlier in 1914), and rehashes them in a lyrical, representational style that is closer to his early fairy-tale-inspired pieces than it is to the bold and challenging work of the pre-war *Compositions.* He wrote to Münter: "All the magnificent power of my old studies is lost." Now, and for the only time in his life, Kandinsky used his fables, his fairy tales, and his visions of Moscow as a curtain to draw down over the horror of the outside world and the inescapable poverty and starvation that were the consequences of war.

Kandinsky in front of his painting *Small Pleasures*

Photograph by Gabriele Münter, *c.* 1913.

Moscow: Red Square

Wassily Kandinsky, 1916

Oil on canvas, 51.5 x 49.5 cm (20½ x 19½ in)

The State Tretyakov Gallery, Moscow

Separation and Denial

Münter added to Kandinsky's physical and material worries by bombarding him with letters. She believed his promises of marriage, pressed him on the issue, and became increasingly hysterical as his letters grew more distant. Kandinsky, typically, veers between anger and guilt. On October 1, 1914 he wrote that her letters "broke his heart," and three months later, on Christmas Day, he wrote again: "lately I have acquired a lot of new grey hairs, and the journey was not to blame. My conscience is troubling me…"

Despite this, he did nothing to help Münter. She owned the Russian house, and had income from her own painting, but emotionally she was abandoned. Two years of pleading letters from her followed; many of them went unanswered. Kandinsky was unwilling to confront the situation. It was almost as though he simply couldn't bear to think of life before the War.

Sweden and the Final Resolution

Finally, in 1916, Kandinsky agreed to meet with Münter in Sweden where she was organizing an exhibition of both their work at the Gummeson Gallery in Stockholm. He appears to have softened towards her at this time and placated her – speaking of the future and eventually promising papers for marriage. It was a terrible and cruel mistake. Münter believed him, and was shocked and grieved when, once again, he stopped replying to her letters. This time, however, the silence was final. As far as she was concerned, he simply disappeared. He never responded to another letter, never personally contacted her, never took pains to explain his actions. They never saw one another again.

It is impossible to say whether Kandinsky raised Münter's hopes because he was a coward, or because he felt one last lift of optimism for the relationship. Most likely the two were intertwined. This did not, however, give Münter any comfort. She quickly realized that Kandinsky had left her behind, but it took her a very long time to forgive him. In her eyes she had renounced "what would have been life, home" for Kandinsky, and she was bitterly rewarded for her sacrifice. Although it took years for Münter to recover from her disappointment, much later in her life she had the generosity of heart to acknowledge that: "He was an idealist and *did not want* to be dishonourable… He failed – and I failed – that's why there was no happy ending."

In 1921, when Kandinsky returned to Germany, his lawyers contacted Münter to ask for his belongings and paintings. She gave some back, but most she kept in her possession, claiming them as "moral damages." Much of the seminal work that he created between 1908 and 1914, Kandinsky never saw again.

Return to Russia

Unlike Münter, it seems that Kandinsky cut his emotional ties with some ease. In March 1916 he returned to Moscow via Petrograd (as St Petersburg had become in 1914). Six months later, in September, he spoke to a young woman on the telephone and fell in love. He immediately painted *To the Unknown Voice*, an homage to this stranger, whose name was Nina Andreevskaja, and arranged to meet her in the Alexander III Museum (today's Pushkin Museum). It marked his return to brave work that pushed at the boundaries of painting. The couple were married in February 1917.

Nina was over 30 years younger than Kandinksy and still a teenager when she married him in a dress that he designed. She was also the opposite of Münter – irrepressible, glamorous, flippant, and a bit silly.

This marriage is perhaps the most surprising episode in Kandinsky's life, and people who met the couple were often surprised by both Nina's charm and her superficiality. Their marriage was, however, supportive and companionable, lasting until Kandinsky's death 27 years later. Despite Nina's support, Kandinsky's life did not settle down. This was nothing to do with Nina and everything to do with timing. In 1917 Russia underwent its Revolution.

To the Unknown Voice

Wassily Kandinsky, 1916

Watercolour and Indian ink on paper, 23.7 x 15.8 cm (9½ x 6 in)

Musée National d'Art Moderne, Centre Georges Pompidou, Paris

Communism

Kandinsky wrote that he "saw the revolution from his window." Despite this, the disruption to his life was not, initially, overwhelming. As a man who believed in social change and saw his art as a moral tool, he fitted well with the Communist ideologies of the Bolshevik regime. Due to his utopian leanings, his fame as the director of Phalanx, author of *Der Blaue Reiter* almanac and *Concerning the Spiritual in Art,* he became a prominent figure in the new order, establishing 22 museums in the four years between 1918 and 1922, delivering numerous lectures, publishing articles, and contributing works for state exhibitions. However, art in the service of society quickly became a divisive issue.

The dominant movement before the Revolution was Suprematism – whose protagonists, most famously Kasimir Malevich, achieved a pure form of abstraction using geometric forms. The Suprematists' ideas were contested by a new movement, Constructivism. Constructivism emerged from a series of debates that ran between 1920 and 1922, which rejected pure abstraction and argued for a more "relevant," functional art, devoid of emotions.

The Constructivists were young and many of them had previously admired Kandinsky and venerated his ideas – he even lived with two of them, Alexander Rodchenko and Varvara Stepanova, and hung their work next to his in the Institute of Artistic Culture, Moscow (INKhUK), of which he was director. However, even this friendship could not prevent Kandinsky's mysticism from seeming increasingly retrograde, even irrelevant. Criticism of his work began to emerge, and it was publicly damned as "arbitrary and individualistic."

Kandinsky, in his usual style, ignored the criticism. In 1920 he produced a program for INKhUK which emphasized intuition, subjectivity, and the occult sciences. It was challenged by the sculptor Aleksei Babichev, who produced a program that focused on the opposite: exact analysis and material organization. In the end neither program was chosen, but the fracas escalated the growing dissent among the Russian avant-garde.

In January 1921 matters came to a head. Kandinksy formally requested a resignation from INKhUK, citing irreconcilable differences, and stating that he felt he "could no longer remain a member."

Strength in Adversity

Despite being sidelined by the Constructivists, Kandinsky was not unhappy during these years. He was in love, and, from 1917, an older and very proud father of a baby boy, Vsedod. Perhaps this is what helped him to maintain the optimism and humour that is apparent in works like *Red Oval,* painted in 1920. Despite the later disagreements, Kandinsky was definitely absorbing the ideas of his younger compatriots. It is a testament to his nature that, despite disagreeing with the younger generation of Russians, he nonetheless learnt from both the sympathetic Suprematists and the antagonistic Constructivists. The composition of *Red Oval* relies on a yellow trapezoid, the shape instantly recognizable as an emblem of Suprematism, the severe geometry broken by the dynamic lines and sense of recession. The visual links between Kandinsky and his compatriots can be seen in a comparison with the work of László Moholy-Nagy, a committed Constructivist.

Although Kandinsky never abandoned a core belief in his pictorial language and his quest for truth, his paintings from this period onwards move towards a more controlled and less spontaneous aesthetic.

László Moholy-Nagy
Chicago A II, 1924

Oil on canvas, 115.8 x 136.5 cm
(45½ x 53½ in)
Solomon R. Guggenheim Museum,
New York

Red Oval
Wassily Kandinsky, 1920
Oil on canvas, 71.5 x 71.2 cm (28 x 28 in)
Solomon R. Guggenheim Museum, New York

Leaving Russia for the Last Time

However, to add to his professional woes, life in Russia was becoming untenable. The Bolshevik takeover led to civil war, and food and money became increasingly scarce. Although the great Russian famine did not begin in earnest until the spring of 1921, in June 1920 Vsedod, only three years old at the time, died of gastroenteritis: the cause was malnutrition. Nina and Kandinksy buried their pain in silence. Although they made yearly trips to his grave, no one else, not even their closest friends, knew that Vsedod had ever existed.

Life also became increasingly subject to bureaucracy. The ideological fist was closing over Russia, and Kandinsky's vision of Moscow was disintegrating before his eyes. Vsedod's death and Kandinsky's resignation from INKhUK were the final straws. He and Nina applied for "a travel permit" for a research trip to Germany and were granted three months' leave. They packed 12 paintings and a few belongings and left. When they did not return, both lost their Russian citizenship. Kandinsky was, once more, an exile.

Levels

Wassily Kandinsky, 1929

Oil on cardboard, 56.6 x 40.6 cm (22 x 16 in)
Solomon R. Guggenheim Museum, New York

An Unexpected Calm

Kandinsky arrived in Berlin to discover that his German savings weren't worth the postage stamp he needed to recover them, and that his weekly stipend was not enough to buy a train ticket from the station to the hotel. Apart from Paul Klee, who lived 186 miles (300 km) away in Weimar (the capital of Germany at the time) – teaching in the underfunded, radical school of art and design, the Bauhaus – his friends were dead or gone. He couldn't get his paintings back from Münter, and all but two of those he'd left with his gallery had been sold, the money already spent. During those first weeks, Nina sold segments of a gold necklace so that they could eat.

Their lifeline came from Klee who – at the behest of the Bauhaus master Walter Gropius – invited Kandinsky to become chair of mural painting there. Although Kandinsky worried that he'd never made a mural in his life, Klee replied that it was of no consequence. The matter was settled.

When Kandinsky arrived in Weimar, Klee took him out to a bar. After counting their marks they realized that they couldn't even afford a coffee, and laughed about it. Thus recommenced a great friendship – a strange friendship in that neither wanted or needed an emotional confidante; they remained self-contained and self-protective. It thrived instead on their shared interest in art and in its teaching. Over the following years they supported and encouraged one another to develop quite different aesthetic and pedagogical theories. Although Kandinsky assumed the role of mentor, the influence ran both ways, and Klee's influence can clearly be seen in Kandinsky's *Levels* of 1929. Their friendship is just one example of the pervasive sense of camaraderie and freedom that characterized the Bauhaus during those years. Unsurprisingly, during these years Kandinsky at last regained a level of contentment. In 1922 he believed that his dream had been realized, declaring: ''the epoch of the Great Spiritual has begun.''

The Bauhaus Years

Kandinsky was, however, closing his eyes to reality. The school was an unlikely success story in a time of profound economic depression and growing political tension. In fact, in 1925 the Bauhaus was forced to move to Dessau after the right-wing local government put pressure on the school, including 50 percent cuts to its funding.

Somehow the spirit of the school was unchecked. In Dessau the sense of ebullience continued. The Klees and Kandinksys shared a Gropius-designed house at Burgkühner Allee 6 (today Stresemannallee) and they were happy. Nina summed up the Bauhaus when she said: "but how could it *not* be a success when it was such fun?"

Among the staff and students at the Bauhaus, Kandinsky cut an eccentric figure. He remained staunchly resistant to the bohemian lifestyle, arriving punctually every day in a suit or, at his most casual, a bow-tie and jacket.

His students viewed him with the kind of reverence normally reserved for shamans or prophets. He was repeatedly described as princely, dignified, and intense. Unlike many of the teachers of the Bauhaus, he was not a friend to the students; he remained aloof, scientific, inspirational. As one of his students related, "Kandinsky didn't conjecture, he declared."

Many of his colleagues found Kandinsky enigmatic. He was clear-sighted and impartial, always called upon in cases of argumentation or dispute, but he spoke rarely of his past. Even Klee and his wife Lily Stumpf knew little of Münter and nothing of Vsedod. A relationship with Kandinsky has been compared to a relationship with a candle: mesmerizing, but never intimate. As his fellow teacher Georg Muche said, "he put seven vests between himself and a cause which meant anything to him…"

Despite the progressive crystallization of his ideas, Kandinsky brought freshness, spark, and irreverence to his teaching, but at the school's famous fancy-dress parties, the best he could do was put on his Bavarian lederhosen while everyone around him embraced eccentricity and excess.

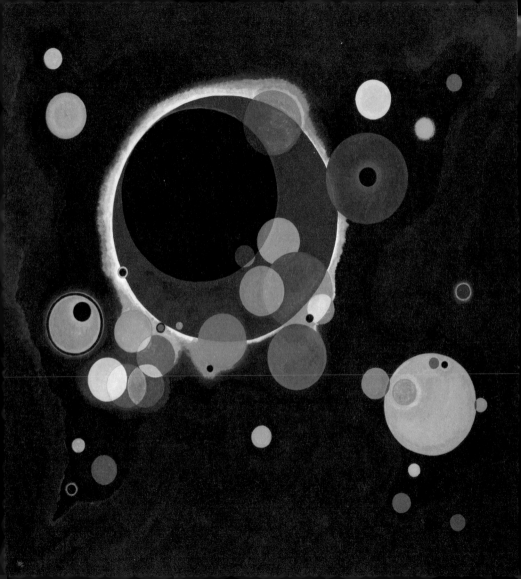

Reason and Magic – Work at the Bauhaus

> Reason and magic are compatible and become one in those things which we call wisdom and consecration, in belief in the stars and in the magic of numbers.
> (Thomas Mann, *Dr. Faustus*)

Mann wrote this passage in response to the writing of Schoenberg who was, in many ways, Kandinsky's intellectual mirror. All three artists discovered the draw of rules and restraints around this time. Perhaps for this reason, the work that Kandinsky produced at the Bauhaus was criticized for its "coldness." Detractors lamented the loss of romance and spontaneity of the earlier abstract pieces. Kandinsky replied with a declaration that he was not abandoning Romanticism, only creating a new language for it by controlling his earlier passion – he likened this to the process of pouring a molten flame into an ice-cold shell.

The circle became the vehicle for his new idea. "I love the circle today as I formerly loved the horse," he said. After the school moved to Dessau, one of the Bauhaus's former students, designer Marcel Breuer, created a set of his famous chairs for the Kandinsky dining room. The chairs were rejected as too square, and Breuer had to make them again, this time with circular seats.

Kandinsky was fairly explicit about his attraction to the circle. It allowed for both restraint and exuberance, being, as he put it, "a synthesis of the greatest paradoxes..." For him, it was also an implicitly silent shape and, as he said: "It happens that at times silence speaks louder than noise."

His work during this time attained a remote, almost crystalline beauty. He began to distance himself from the expressive, Romantic element of his work. His art, like his character, was manifesting what he recalled as a "great calm" that had descended on him during his years in Russia.

Wassily and Nina Kandinsky sitting in the dining room of their apartment at the Bauhaus.
Photograph by Lucia Moholy, silver gelatin print from a glass negative, 1927.
Bauhaus-Archiv, Berlin.

Revelry and mischief were important aspects of life at the Bauhaus. For Klee's 50th birthday a group of students hired a plane from the nearby Junkers air factory to drop an angel-shaped package of presents into Klee and Kandinsky's garden. They missed, the parachute didn't open properly, and the angel crashed through the roof sending Marianne Brandt and Marcel Breuer designs smashing into the house.

The Total Work of Art

Kandinsky never lost the dream of artistic immersion initially inspired by the houses in Vologda. Although no such project ever came to fruition, he was much inspired by Wagner's idea of the Gesamtkunstwerk or "total work of art." During the Bauhaus years he started to work towards it, experimenting with new art forms, designing textiles, painting furniture, and writing abstract plays that he called "scenic compositions." One of the most renowned is *Der Gelbe Klang (Yellow Sound)*, a play with no narrative or reference to external forms that was, perhaps unsurprisingly, not performed during his lifetime.

While at the Bauhaus, Kandinsky also produced a pared-down, almost surreal set for Modest Mussorgsky's *Pictures at an Exhibition* in 1928, and a rather wonderful ceramic-tiled music room for Deutsche Bauausstellung in 1931. His most important work, however, is lost to us. They were the so-called "murals" for the Juryfreie Show in 1922 (see recreation opposite) which he created with the help of the students from his mural department. The finished cycle of paintings was not only a re-imagining of art, it was a re-imagining of space. Kandinksy dissolved the boundaries of the room with canvases that he propped against the wall. His creation was at odds with the functionalism of the Bauhaus, and it was the first emergence of an idea that was only realized with the rise of installation art.

View of the *"Salon Juryfreie"*

Reconstructed by Jean Vidal using the five original
gouaches executed by Kandinsky in 1922. This view shows the
exhibition at the Palazzo Reale in Milan, December 13, 2013,

Success

During his three years at Dessau, Kandinsky thrived. He relished the greater access to nature and started to produce new and influential work and teaching theories. Nine German collectors founded the Kandinsky Society in 1925 to buy paintings from the artist as a form of financial support. In May of 1926 a major retrospective was organized at Braunschweig Castle to celebrate his 60th birthday. Among other places, he exhibited his work in Dusseldorf at the Great Art Exhibition, in Dresden, at the International Art Exhibition in Berlin, at the Great Berlin Art Exhibition and, importantly, for the first time in Paris at Galerie Zak in January 1929 – he was filled with energy and drive.

Just before the school's move from Weimar in 1925, Galka Scheyer, an old friend from Munich, approached Kandinsky, Klee, and two other artists associated with the Blue Rider exhibitions. She had a commercial proposition: that they reunite as "The Blue Four" and that Scheyer – who moved to New York the same year – would be their promoter and agent. They agreed. The financial situation was sufficiently desperate that Kandinsky was happy to be paid in tinned food whenever Scheyer sold a painting.

At the beginning the sale of paintings was rare, but over time Scheyer's promotion and lectures helped to raise his profile so that by 1930 he was visited in Dessau by both Marcel Duchamp and the great American collector Solomon Guggenheim.

Poster for Kandinsky exhibition celebrating his 60th birthday, 1926.
Offset lithography printed in colour, by Herbert Bayer,
48.2 x 63.5 cm (19 x 25 in).
Museum of Modern Art, New York.

Tragedy

Although the Kandinskys were happy at the Bauhaus, tragedy soon struck again. They should have seen it coming. Ten years earlier it was foreshadowed in an argument with their friend, Schoenberg. In April 1923 Kandinsky asked Schoenberg to teach at the Bauhaus. Schoenberg's response was acrid. He wrote that taking a job at the Bauhaus was pointless because, as a Jew, he'd learnt in recent months, "that I am not a German, not a European, indeed perhaps scarcely even a human being, but I am a Jew." He went on to say that reports had reached him that Kandinsky was something of an anti-Semite. Kandinsky's response was heart-felt but teasing, almost unbelieving. He dismissed the reports, assured his friend that he loved him "as an artist and a human being," and – apart from writing that "nationality is a matter of the greatest indifference to me" – more or less glossed over the issue.

He had misread the situation. Nationality was not a matter of general indifference across Europe in the 1920s, as Kandinsky was to learn. Schoenberg replied with a long, pained, and heart-wrenching tirade. It was utterly unforgiving: he cut off the friendship, claiming that Kandinsky was no longer his friend, nor the man he had once known. Kandinsky was devastated. He showed the letter to Gropius who paled and immediately blamed it on internecine Bauhaus politics.

Wherever the fault lay, and whatever actually happened, Kandinsky still did not heed the implications. He took it as a personal affair and closed his eyes to the signs in German society at large that his Bauhaus paradise was bound to shatter. In 1928 he and Nina became German citizens and threw a costume party to celebrate. In 1929 the stock market crashed. Kandinsky was offered a teaching post in New York but he turned it down. Two years later the Nazis closed down the Bauhaus outpost at Dessau. Although Mies van der Rohe re-opened the school in a derelict factory in Berlin late in 1932, the Gestapo closed it for the last time in April of the following year. Under increasing political pressure and an atmosphere of extremism and violence, Kandinsky became a target of the new regime, both because he was a Russian, and because he was associated with the liberal Bauhaus, which was deemed a "Communist threat." In 1933 Kandinsky, who'd followed the school to Berlin, finally confronted the inevitable and fled once again, this time to Paris, where he arrived in January 1934. He was now nearly 70 years old.

Making Peace with Science

Paris in the 1930s must have seemed a pale imitation of the bustling modern metropolis that Kandinsky had known before World War I. The buildings were uncared for, the roads deserted and dirty, the museums empty. Kandinsky, however, found an apartment away from the dilapidated centre, in the newly built modern and wealthy suburb of Neuilly-sur-Seine. He lived on Boulevard de Seine, 135 (today's Boulevard du Général Koenig), in a light and airy apartment with views of the river from no less than three sitting rooms.

Kandinsky fought these upheavals in his life with the same remarkable optimism that coloured his work in the final, heavy days of the fight with the Constructivists in Russia 13 years before. This time, however, humour is replaced with a withdrawn, almost meditative quality. The effect on his painting was the dawn of the uplifting luminosity that is exhibited in *Graceful Ascent* (1934).

In the last years at the Bauhaus, Kandinsky had started to consult biological dictionaries. Subsequently in Paris he collected images from science journals, articles on natural history, and books on zoology and embryology. He collated a huge archive of pictures that consisted mainly of amoebas, marine invertebrates, larvae, embryos, and extinct or exotic animals. Their biomorphic forms begin to appear in his paintings around 1936 – for example *Capricious Forms* (see overleaf), where he juxtaposes the high-minded circles and quadrilaterals of the Bauhaus years with primordial, biomorphic shapes, entwining them across the canvas in a surreal floating world of pastel pinks, greens, and yellows.

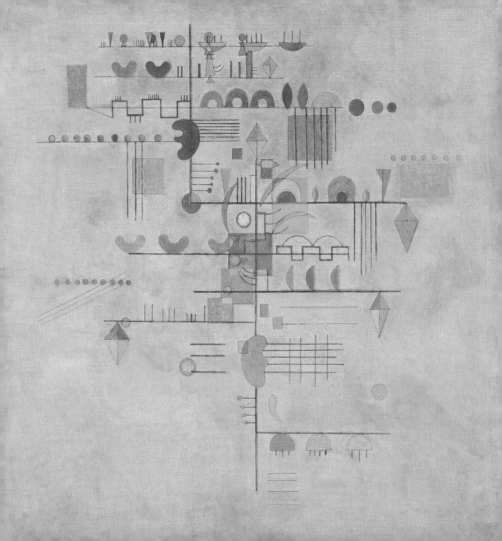

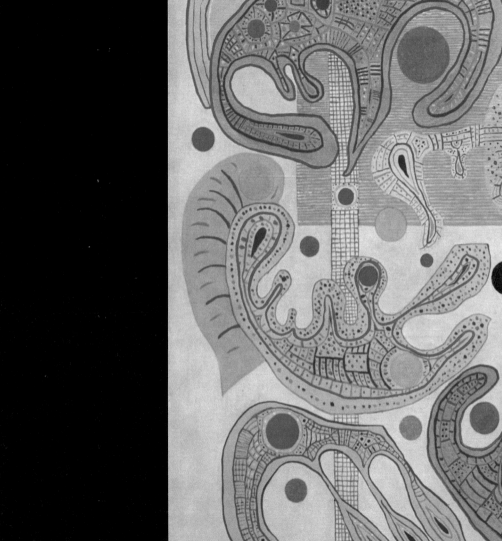

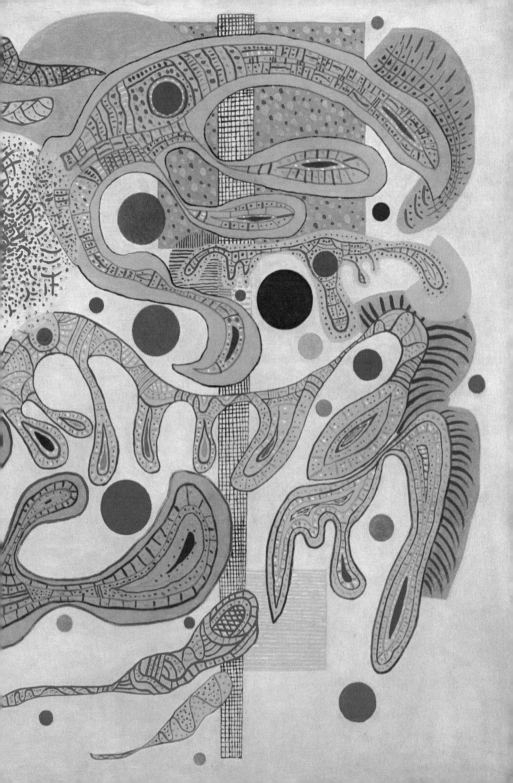

Retreat

Kandinsky's life in Paris was, from an external point of view, mundane. On arrival, he was greeted by leading Parisian artists – it was Marcel Duchamp who found the apartment in Neuilly, and the Kandinskys were initially in touch with Fernand Léger, Robert and Sonia Delaunay, Joan Miró, Man Ray, and Max Ernst. Over time, however, he gently shed their company, and limited his circle to Hans Arp and Sophie Taeuber-Arp, Alberto Magnelli, Piet Mondrian, and André Breton.

The younger artists and journalists who made the effort to visit him at his home were often disappointed. What they found was not a revolutionary or a prophet but a pleasant, rather distant figure. As he sank away from chattering humanity, so his work became increasingly peaceful. It did not have the raw energy and romance of the great pre-1914 works, nor the precision and control of his Bauhaus period. It used biomorphism but seemed to ascend to a place that exists beyond science, and also beyond language. Kandinsky finally laid down his pen in 1940. The lightheartedness of organic shapes in *Capricious Forms* is distilled to a pictorial language that emits quiet and stillness. *Sky Blue* contains a universe within its bounds and reconciles Kandinsky's two overriding preoccupations: science and the unknown. He had finally learnt the lesson of the circle: he embraced the silence that he was so proud not only to hear, but also, finally, to appreciate.

Sky Blue
Wassily Kandinsky, 1940

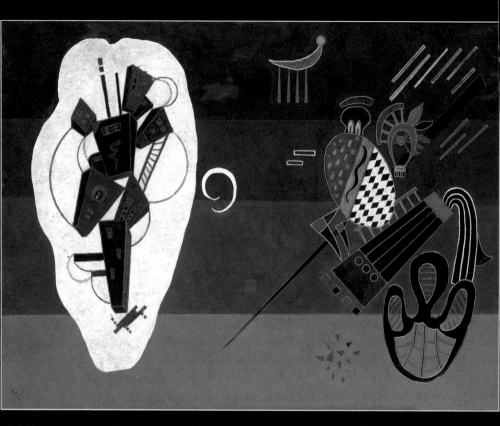

Isolation

Wassily Kandinsky, 1944

Oil on canvas, 42 x 58 cm (16½ x 23 in)

Helly Nahmad Gallery, New York

Resolution

Although Kandinsky stayed very mentally active in Paris, he ceased to travel. Not only was travel difficult due to international tensions, but he no longer felt the draw of it. His last trip was in 1931, to Switzerland for a final visit to Klee, who was dying. After that he entrenched himself in Neuilly and committed himself simply to staying. He defiantly told his friends that he would have no part in the conflict:

> National anthems have now been sung in almost all countries. But I am content not to be a singer… these national anthems are precisely a type of lure.

In 1937 Kandinsky was one of the artists most prominently represented in the infamous Nazi Degenerate Art Exhibition. In 1938 the Kandinskys' German passports ran out and they chose not to renew them. In 1939 they received French citizenship, and in the same year the Nazis burnt 4,000 "degenerate" works of art, including Kandinsky's first three great *Compositions*. As an ex-member of the "Socialist" Bauhaus, a fugitive from the late '30s, and a listed "degenerate," Kandinsky was in very real danger. His friends begged him to flee to the US, where there was a thriving community of artists, and where he'd been offered asylum. At 74 though, he'd had enough of running away. The decision to stay was somewhat foolhardy. It was also immensely brave.

The Nazis entered Paris in 1940. By sheer luck and the vagaries of fate the Germans left the couple in peace. The Kandinskys were ignored due to a listing error that overlooked their "Bolshevik" and "degenerate" status. Kandinsky, blissfully unperturbed, confined himself to his house, away from the horrors of war and the regrets of the past, and sank further and further into his painting. Any remaining concern about the stigmas of decorativeness and illustration evaporate from the last works, which radiate a life-affirming pleasure in colour and form. The very last paintings, such as *Isolation*, are some of his greatest.

On Kandinsky's 78th birthday in 1944 his few remaining friends rallied together and somehow rustled up champagne, chocolates, and cigars in ration-starved Nazi-occupied Paris. At the celebration there was an air of hope. There was vague talk of a possible return to Moscow, and Nina speculated about a ceasefire in Paris. Kandinsky was in high spirits and recited his favourite Pushkin poem. The next day he felt tired, and told Nina he would stay in bed. Not wanting to break the habit of a lifetime, he did not call for a doctor. A couple of days later he died in his sleep.

He left behind an extraordinary legacy of painting, poetry, pedagogy, and theory. Most of all, for a man tormented by the impossible ambition to arrive at some kind of truth, he seems to have finally achieved the happiness that he hints at in his own question:

> Ask yourself whether a work of art has carried you to a world unknown to you before. If you find that it has, what more could you want?

At the end, as throughout his adult life, art was his only solution, his only route to peace and happiness. Jean Arp, one of the friends at the final party, wrote a few lines that Kandinksy would surely have considered the finest kind of eulogy:

> His work is aglow with spiritual reality… Things blossom, sparkle, ripple in his paintings and poems. They speak of old blood and young stones.

Kandinsky painting in his studio, 1936
Black and white photograph
Private collection

Glossary

ABSTRACT Expressing ideas and emotions by using elements such as colors and lines without attempting to create a realistic picture; having only intrinsic form with little or no attempt at pictorial representation or narrative content.

AESTHETIC Of, relating to, or dealing with art or the beautiful; artistic; pleasing in appearance; attractive; appreciative of, responsive to, or zealous about the beautiful; responsive to or appreciative of what is pleasurable to the senses.

AVANT-GARDE A group of people who develop new and often very surprising ideas in art, literature, etc.

BAUHAUS Of, relating to, or influenced by a school of design noted especially for a program that synthesized technology, craftsmanship, and design aesthetics.

BIOMORPHIC Resembling or suggesting the forms of living organisms.

BOURGEOIS Relating to or belonging to the middle class of society; having qualities or values associated with the middle class; too concerned about wealth, possessions, and respectable behavior.

CONSTRUCTIVISM A nonobjective art movement originating in Russia and concerned with formal organization of planes and expression of volume in terms of modern industrial materials (as glass and plastic).

ECCENTRICITY The quality of being strange or unusual in behavior; an act or habit that is strange or unusual; deviation from an established pattern or norm; odd or whimsical behavior.

ESOTERIC Only taught to or understood by members of a special group; hard to understand; limited to a small number of people; of special, rare, or unusual interest.

FAUVE A painter practicing Fauvism, a movement in painting typified by the work of Matisse and characterized by vivid colors, free treatment of form, and a resulting vibrant and decorative effect.

MATERIALISM A way of thinking that gives too much importance to material possessions rather than to spiritual or intellectual things; a doctrine that the only or the highest values or objectives lie in material well-being and in the furtherance of material progress.

MYSTICISM The belief that direct knowledge of God, spiritual truth, or ultimate reality can be attained through subjective experience (as intuition or insight); the experience of mystical union or direct communion with ultimate reality.

PROFANE To treat (something sacred) with abuse, irreverence, or contempt; desecrate; to debase by a wrong, unworthy, or vulgar use.

PROPHET One who utters divinely inspired revelations; one regarded by a group of followers as the final authoritative revealer of God's will; one gifted with more than ordinary spiritual and moral insight; an inspired poet; one who foretells future events; an effective or leading spokesman for a cause, doctrine, or group.

RATIONALISM A theory that reason is in itself a source of knowledge superior to and independent of sense perceptions; a view that reason and experience rather than the nonrational are the fundamental criteria in the solution of problems; reliance on reason as the basis for establishment of religious truth.

ROMANTICISM A literary, artistic, and philosophical movement originating in the eighteenth century, characterized chiefly by a reaction against neoclassicism and an emphasis on the imagination and emotions.

SHAMAN A priest or priestess who uses magic for the purpose of curing the sick, divining the hidden, and controlling events; one who resembles a shaman; a high priest.

SUBJECTIVITY Peculiar to a particular individual; personal; modified or affected by personal views, experience, or background; arising from conditions within the brain or sense organs and not directly caused by external stimuli; arising out of or identified by means of one's perception of one's own states and processes.

SUPREMATIST Practitioner of an early 20th century art movement in Russia producing abstract works featuring flat geometric forms.

SYMBOLIST One of a group of writers and artists in France after 1880 reacting against realism, concerning themselves with general truths instead of actualities, exalting the metaphysical and the mysterious, and aiming to unify and blend the arts and the functions of the senses.

SYNAESTHESIA A subjective sensation or image of a sense (as of color) other than the one (as of sound) being stimulated.

THEOSOPHY Teaching about God and the world based on mystical insight; the teachings of a modern movement originating in the United States in 1875 and following chiefly Buddhist and Brahmanic theories especially of pantheistic evolution and reincarnation.

For More Information

The Getty

1200 Getty Center Drive

Los Angeles, CA 90049-1679

(310) 440-7300

Website: http://www.getty.edu

The J. Paul Getty Trust is a cultural and philanthropic institution dedicated to the presentation, conservation, and interpretation of the world's artistic legacy. The Getty is dedicated to the proposition that works of art are windows onto the world's diverse and intertwined histories, mirrors of humanity's innate imagination and creativity, and inspiration to envision the future.

The Museum of Modern Art (MoMA)

11 West 53rd Street

New York, NY 10019

(212) 708-9400

Website: https://www.moma.org

Founded in 1929 as an educational institution, The Museum of Modern Art is dedicated to being the foremost museum of modern art in the world. Through the leadership of its Trustees and staff, The Museum of Modern Art manifests this commitment by establishing, preserving, and documenting a permanent collection of the highest order that reflects the vitality, complexity, and unfolding patterns of modern and contemporary art and by presenting exhibitions and educational programs of unparalleled significance. Central to The Museum of Modern Art's mission is the encouragement of an ever-deeper understanding and enjoyment of modern and contemporary art by the diverse local, national, and international audiences that it serves.

WEBSITES

Because of the changing nature of internet links, Rosen Publishing has developed an online list of websites related to the subject of this book. This site is updated regularly. Please use this link to access this list:

http://www.rosenlinks.com/LGA/kandinsky

For Further Reading

Barnett, Vivian Endicott, et al. *Klee and Kandinsky: Neighbors, Friends, Rivals.* London, England, Prestel, 2015.

Becks-Malorny, Ulrike. *Kandinsky.* Cologne, Germany: Taschen, 2007.

Benjamin, Roger, and Cristina Ashjian. *Kandinsky and Klee in Tunisia.* Oakland, CA: University of California Press, 2015.

Benson, Timothy O. *Expressionism in Germany and France: From Van Gogh to Kandinsky.* London, England: Prestel, 2014.

Duchting, Hajo. *Kandinsky.* Cologne, Germany: Taschen, 2015.

Henry, Michel, and Scott Davidson. *Seeing the Invisible: On Kandinsky.* New York, NY: Bloomsbury Academic, 2009.

Kandinsky, Wassily. *Concerning the Spiritual in Art.* Las Vegas, NV: Empire Art Press, 2013.

Kandinsky, Wassily. *Kandinsky.* New York, NY: Parkstone Press, 2016.

Lampe, Angela, et al. *Kandinsky: A Retrospective.* New Haven, CT: Yale University Press, 2014.

Sers, Philippe. *Kandinsky: The Elements of Art.* New York, NY: Thames & Hudson, 2016.

Bibliography

Boissel, J., and N. Weber. *Albers and Kandinsky: Friends in Exile, a Decade of Correspondence, 1929–1940.* New Haven, CT: Yale University Press, 2015.

Schoenberg, Arnold, and Wassily Kandinsky. *Arnold Schoenberg/Wassily Kandinsky: Letters, Pictures, and Documents.* Edited by Jelena Hahl-Koch. Translated by John C. Crawford. New York, NY: Faber & Faber, 1984.

Hoberg, Annegret. *Kandinsky and Münter: Letters and Reminiscences, 1902–1914.* New York, NY: Prestel, 2005.

Kandinsky, Wassily. *The Blaue Reiter Almanac.* New York, NY: Thames & Hudson, 1974.

Kandinsky, Wassily. *Concerning the Spiritual in Art.* Mineola, NY: Dover, 1977.

Lindsay, Kenneth C., and Peter Vergo. *Kandinsky: Complete Writings on Art.* Translated by Michael Sadler. Boston, MA: Da Capo, 1994.

Weber, Nicholas Fox. *The Bauhaus Group: Six Masters of Modernism.* New Haven, CT: Yale University Press, 2011.

Weiss, Peg. *Kandinsky and Old Russia: The Artist as Ethnographer and Shaman.* New Haven, CT Yale University Press, 1995.

Weiss, Peg. *Kandinsky in Munich: The Formative Jugendstil Years.* Princeton, NJ: Princeton University Press, 1979.

Index